I0787504

Anxiety Journal

A Step by Step Guided Journal to Live free from Anxiety in 30 Days or Less

Copyright © 2021 Psyche Guidance

All rights reserved

No part of this book may be reproduced, or stored in a retrieval system, or transmitted in any form or by any means, electronic, mechanical, photocopying, recording, or otherwise, without express written permission of the publisher.

ISBN: 9798715699930

"Nobody can bring you peace but
yourself."

—*Ralph Waldo Emerson*

Introduction

Living a life free from anxiety is something that you need.

Life is dark when you are always anxious and stressed.

 What you need is some guidance, solutions, and of course being positive and expecting good results. And this is exactly what I'm going to help to achieve in this guided journal.

What you should also know is that your anxiety can be cured, or at least can be reduced. So in this journal, I will make my effort to give you the best advice and the best guide, and healing writing prompts that work for you.

Welcome to this journey of anxiety relief, and as you had the decision to get and use this journal, that means you have the decision to change to feel more powerful in your life, and all that means you deserve that change that you will get.

During this journey I want you to treat me as a friend that you trust to guides you. This journal is not just a notebook that makes you express yourself for a moment, but it is a method and process that will help you a lot. So please treat me as a friend.

If you want to get more efficient results during this writing journey, I have some useful tips for you. These tips are optional, but they are so recommended if you want to enjoy your journaling and especially get the results that you want.

Have a Suitable Place:

Look for a place that makes you relaxed and focused, and avoid the places of noises or where you cannot be concentrated. You can go to a room in your house, or you can also journal outside like in a cafe or library.

 It is good to journal always in the same place because if you trained your mind about always do a thing in the same place it will become a habit, and you will be attached to this habit whenever you get there.

Listen to Soft Music in the Background:

 Music is also a tool for psychological therapy. For me, it helps me to stay focused and live with my thoughts and emotions during writing, but if music makes your focus less, you can journal without it.

If you like journaling with music; I recommend listening to soft or classical music. But avoid hard songs like Hip Hop or Metal songs.

 I recommend also listening to the same piece of music or the same playlist because when you do that, you train your mind to start journaling whenever you listen to it again.

Candles:

Candles give a good mood in the environment of your writing place. It helps you to focus more, gives you a romantic mood, makes you feel relaxed, and engaged in your writing.

Coffee or Tea:

I don't know why I'm giving this kind of advice, LOL. I just love drinking coffee during doing something creative like journaling, because also helps me to focus.

If you are ready, let's go!

UNDERSTANDING ANXIETY

"Any fool can know. The point is to understand."
— Albert Einstein

1 - Why you should First Understand Anxiety?

Understanding the problem will help you to solve it. I know that you know that feeling of anxiety and how bad it is and how it makes you feel.

But if you want to defeat your enemy you should know him. You should understand his tricks and his points of weaknesses so you can defeat him.

The same thing goes with anxiety. So you should study anxiety scientifically and spiritually so you can know how to heal yourself.

2 – What is Anxiety?

What I'm going to explain to you here is not something from dictionary or scientific or psychological definition. There are a lot of resources if you want to study and know about that.

But what I'm going to give you is small definition, so you can understand it without complication.

Anxiety is when you are in a "dangerous" situation, and then you feel stressed about it.

THAT'S IT!

Or if you want a scientific definition, is an emotion characterized by feelings of tension, worried thoughts and physical changes like increased blood pressure.

That's a definition from the American Psychological Assosiation.

3 - Anxiety vs Fear

- **The common thing between Anxiety and Fear:**

They are both alerting signals that your brain in certain situations.

- **BUT:**

Anxiety is a generalized response to an unknown threat or internal conflict.

Fear is focused on known external danger.

4 - How you can treat Anxiety using this book

Most of advices that I'm going to give you is by writing, I'm going to ask you some questions and give you some prompts that will help you understand yourself and your anxiety more, and this will change your mindset, and the way you think, and also take the required action.

I have also some CBT and NLP exercises for you that will help you in a magical way to deal with your anxiety and calm it.

A COACHING SESSION
WITH YOU

1 – How I can coach you with your Anxiety

In this section of this book, I will coach you in the way that most of life coaches do. And that is the grow model.

GROW Stands for:

- **G**OAL
- **R**EALITY
- **O**PTIONS
- **W**ill do

LET'S FIRST UNDERSTAND AND KNOW YOUR PROBLEM AND YOUR GOAL…

Answer these questions:

How do you Define Anxiety?

. . . .
. . . .
. . . .
. . . .
. . . .
. . . .
. . . .
. . . .
. . . .
. . . .
. . . .

Describe the feeling when you are anxious.

When/What are the moments that make you feel Anxious?

What are the Other Problems and Consequences that Anxiety had in your Life?

Express your Hope that you will get rid soon of Anxiety.

NOW LET'S DISCOVER YOUR REALITY...

What did you have already tried?

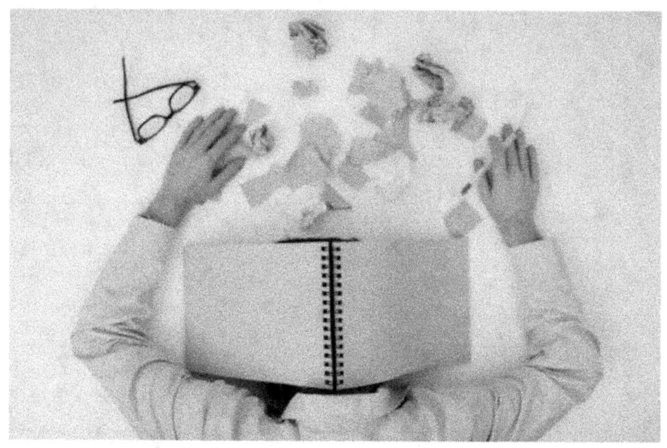

Is it hard for you to calm your Anxiety? If yes, then why?

What are the reasons that you think it stops you from getting rid of Anxiety?

What are the things **you cannot control** in your life that causes you Anxiety? (Write it down and don't focus on it because it is out of your control.)

NOW LET'S DISCOVER YOUR OPTIONS...

What are the options you have in your life that you are just **lazy** to practice?

What did you already have tried and it gave you some results?

LET'S TAKE ACTION...

List some of the things you can do to calm your anxiety.

Do you feel sometimes lazy to practice things that can help you (like meditation or going for a walk)? IF YES, **How do you think you can fix that?**

What are the **little actions** you can do for the short term and you will **commit to it**?

Write some repetitive affirmation phrases that says you will commit to it.

Start at least with Mini-Habits

If we take the habit of meditation for example, and supposing that you do not practice meditation. You think that you should start with one hour a day.

That's a huge mistake you can do.

Always start with mini habits; it can be just for less than 10 minute a day.

If you start your habit of meditation by one hour a day, it will be boring, so as a result you will stop. So remember to start small.

The same thing goes with any good habit you want to build.

Neuro-Linguistic Programming (NLP)

What is NLP?

Neuro-Linguistic Programming is a pseudoscientific approach used in self-help and psychotherapy created by John Grinder and Richard Bandler in California, in the 1970s

Neuro: (your thinking process) the way you use your senses to understand what's happening around you.

Linguistic: (the words you use) How you use language and how it influences you and those around you. It can be verbally or non verbally.

Programming: (your behavior) how you organize your ideas and reactions, and how it affects you and others.

Maybe you know what NLP is exactly, but for those who are complicated about the real meaning of it, this is some simple bullet point definitions:

NLP is a tool to make a change to live a better life.

NLP is a tool to change thoughts, beliefs, mindset... (Programming your mind)

The way of programming is using a LANGUAGE that your mind understands.

Your mind should affect your outer world.

The language that your mind understands is usually IMAGINATION techniques or something that make you mind take action.

You can practice NLP by yourself or with a professional.

How NLP can help you

NLP can help you a lot and change your life in any area.

When it comes to anxiety or any problem with the state of emotions, NLP can help you change it with simple tricks and exercises.

And that's what you will learn in the next few pages.

NLP Exercices

Most of NLP practices are by visualizing, but in the next few pages you will use visualization with writing so it will be more effective.

Not all the exercises that I will give are by writing, there are some practices that will help you by using your imagination.

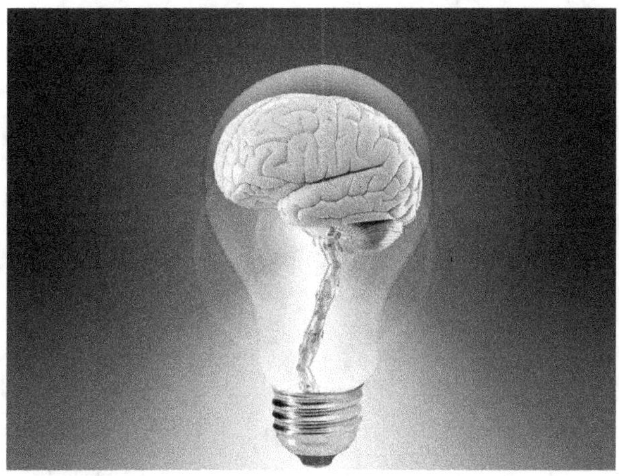

Write a positive goal about living a life free from Anxiety.

Positive goal means that you a goal of achieving something, not not achieving something. For example your goal should succeeding not prevent failing.

Edit your Mental Image.

Your mind works like a computer, so you can edit some data in it. And the data that you have in your mind are memories, thoughts, words, etc. If they are negative, that means you should edit it to positive ones.

Thinking about things like people, events, or other things can help you understand how you feel about them. I will give you an exercise for you to practice.

Move to a quiet and silent place. Relax and imagine things or people that make you feel anxious, and then imagine them turning darker and moving further and further away.

You can practice this exercise also if you want to change emotions for the better. You can imagine things or people that make you feel positive turning brighter and coming closer to you.

After this exercise write how you this made you feel.

....
....
....
....
....
....
....
....
....
....
....
....
....

Mess with negative voices in your head.

We all speak to ourselves in the mind. And this internal dialogue can be positive or it can be negative. And this has a lot to do with your anxiety level. So notice how you speak to yourself.

If you noticed that you have a negative talk in your mind like "I can't speak to people," or "I'm afraid," repeat the message but with a distorted sound. You can make it sound like a goofy cartoon character, like Donald Duck or Spongebob.

And write how this made you feel.

Play Out Scenarios Backward.

As I said before your mind is like a computer, and imagine that in that computer there is a movie, that movie contains a bad experience that makes you feel anxious. So what you are going to do is editing that movie by playing out the scenarios backward.

If there is a bad experience in your life that makes you feel anxious when you think about it, treat it like a movie. What you are going to do is playing it backward, starting from after it occurred and then to right before it occurred. Repeat this many times so you can memories the backward sequence. And don't forget to make a different ending on that makes you feel okay or happier.

Visualize Colors and Connect them with feelings

Let's say for example you want to become confident. Now you know "confidence" what it means. But if I asked you what is the color of confidence? I know that my question looks stupid, but in reality, our mind can imagine a color of something invisible.

For example, you can imagine love is red, or you can imagine forgiveness is white. Any feeling you know you can imagine that he has a color. Now if you want to feel confident, you can imagine a color that looks confident to you, such black. Imagine a black square and step into it. Imagine exactly how it would and feel to be in that square

Practice that on calmness feelings and write how this made you feel.

....

....

....

....

....

....

....

....

....

....

....

....

....

Anchoring

Anchoring is something that all of us go through, and I think that maybe is something that we experience almost everyday.

Have you ever were listening to a song a long time ago, and when you decided to listen to it again, you start feeling and remembering the memories that you had back then that time when you were listening to that song? Have you ever experienced that?

 That is exactly anchoring, and it is not just working with songs, it can work with smells, views, tastes, etc. So how we can use anchoring as an NLP practice to improve our mental health.

First, there is an exercise you should do, or do at least once. I'm going to give an example of confidence, but this exercise works in any feelings you want to experience like calmness or joy.

If you want to be confident for example I want you to sit and relax, then think in a moment that you were super confident, and then try to take a position with your hands or fingers, it can be any position you want, but it should be simple like putting your hand on your chest or a position with just your fingers.

If you repeat that exercise what will happen is your mind will habituate when you make that position that you choose. It will give you the feelings of the moment that you were thinking in.

COGNITIVE BEHAVIORAL THERAPY (CBT)

The meaning of CBT

To give you a simple definition, cognitive behavioral therapy is type of treatment (therapy) done by changing the way you think (cognitive) and behave (behavioral).

How CBT can be Effective for your Anxiety.

CBT can help you change the negative thought patterns so you can improve the way you feel. Also it will break the cycles that makes you feel anxious by changing your behaviors.

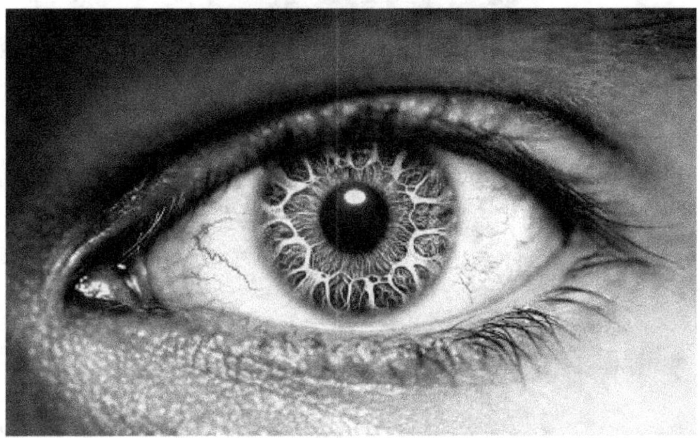

IDENTIFYING YOUR THOUGHTS (COGNITIVE)

What are the thoughts that Makes you Anxious?

....
....
....
....
....
....
....
....
....
....
....
....
....
....

Are most of your thoughts negative?

Write each thought you usually have, and mention how it makes you feel.

Write each negative thought you have and Exchange it with Positive Ones by your Written Words.

....
....
....
....
....
....
....
....
....
....
....
....
....
....
....
....

IDENTIFYING YOUR BEHAVIOUR

What are the things that you are doing that might be are causes of your Anxiety?

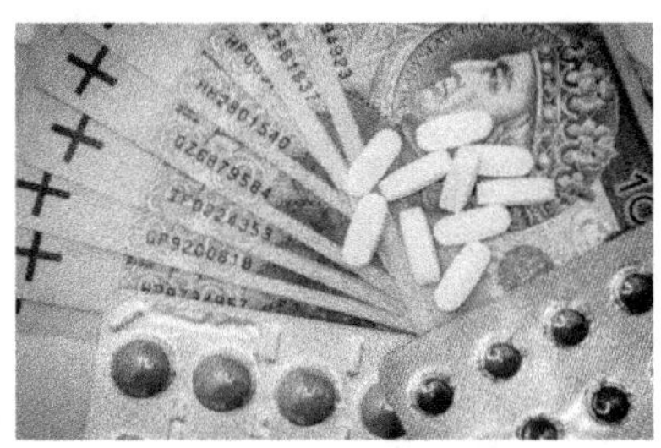

....
....
....
....
....
....
....
....
....
....
....
....
....
....
....
....
....

How you can change that behavior?

Write some repetitive affirmation phrases that says you will commit to it.

BONUS: INSPIRATIONAL PROMPTS

Today, I am thankful for

My favorite accomplishment is

II felt sad when

What is one thing I wish I could change

My happiest memory is

What's been bugging me lately?

Make a list of 15 things you love about yourself

One way I could love myself more is

My Childhood hero was __________ and I am similar to them in these ways:

What is your best quality?

Write a letter to one of your parents. (You do not have to give it to them.)

Make a list of 10 quotes that inspire you

And Finally, Make a list of 20 things you are grateful for.

Before you leave

Thank you for having this journey with me, and be someone who opens his heart with his written words. I hope that this journaling journey had an impact on your psyche, and it gives you a charge to relieve your anxiety and more energized to live your life fully and happily.

There are a lot of promises that gave yourself during this journey. So the thing that I wish is that you took action as much as you can.

I'd want to know about your experience with this journal, so if you don't mind, please tell me how your journey was great and the progress that you had in the reviews of Amazon.

Thank you my friend!

Previous Kindle Ebooks :

Journals :

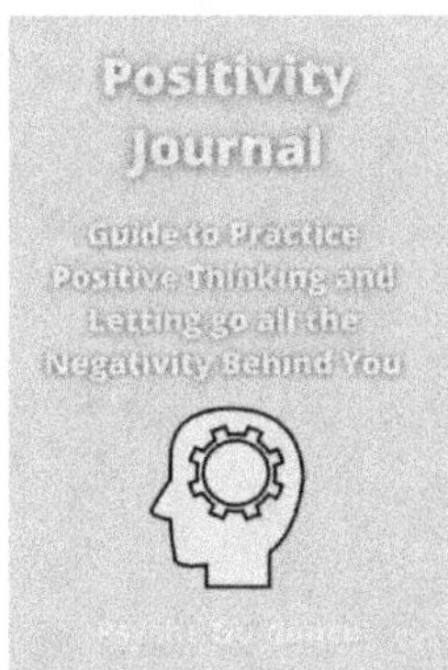

Let it Go
Journal
A Journal for Leaving
Your Pain Behind
and Creating a Happy Life

Copyright © 2021 Psyche Guidance

www.ingramcontent.com/pod-product-compliance
Lightning Source LLC
Chambersburg PA
CBHW071231240726
48654CB00009B/992